What's in this book

This book belongs to

T0351537

_____

城市设计师 City designer

学习内容 Contents

沟通 Communication

说说公共建筑和设施
Talk about public
buildings and facilities

背景介绍：
大人和小孩正在设计城市。

生词 New words

⭐	学校	school
⭐	图书馆	library
⭐	商店	shop
⭐	超市	supermarket
⭐	医院	hospital
⭐	火车站	train station
⭐	或者	either, or
⭐	公园	park
	设计	to design
	邮局	post office
	体育馆	gymnasium
	电影院	cinema
	银行	bank

句式 Sentence patterns

我们还可以设计体育馆、医院或者火车站。

We can also design gymnasiums, hospitals or train stations.

别忘了公园或者电影院。

Don't forget parks or cinemas.

跨学科学习 Project

设计未来环保城市
Design a green city of the future

文化 Cultures

世界各地古典的公共建筑
Classical public buildings around the world

Get ready

1 Do you think the city you live in is well designed and has good facilities?

2 What is your favourite part of the city?

3 Is there anything that you would improve? Why?

故事大意：
通过问题引导学生思考作为小设计师，他们想设计怎样的城市，有哪些公共建筑和设施，以及它们给城市带来哪些方便等问题。

shè jì
设计

如果你是城市设计师，你会怎样设计你的城市呢？

参考问题和答案：

1 Do you like the girl's design? (Yes, I like the modern buildings. No, there are not enough trees.)

2 How would you design your city if you were a city designer? (I would design a modern city/a big city/a green city.)

xué xiào
学校

tú shū guǎn
图书馆

你想设计更大的学校和图书馆吗？
更多的学生可以在那里学习。

POST OFFICE

yóu jú
邮局

shāng diàn
商店

chāo shì
超市

你想设计更多的邮局、商店和超市吗？我们的生活会更方便。

参考问题和答案：

1 Do you know where the post office, the shops and the supermarket are in your community? (Yes./No.)
2 Is your community convenient? (Yes, life is quite easy./No, because I live on a farm.)

tǐ yù guǎn
体育馆

yī yuàn
医院

"或者"用于肯定句，指在可供选择的东西、状况或过程中的挑选。如：他想学数学或者学地理。

huò zhě
或者

huǒ chē zhàn
火车站

参考问题和答案：
What facility would you want for your city, a gymnasium, a hospital or a train station? (A gymnasium, because we do not have one yet./A new train station, because the one we have is too old.)

我们还可以设计体育馆、医院或者火车站，让设施更全面。

gōng yuán
公园

diàn yǐng yuàn
电影院

别忘了公园或者电影院。休息时，大家都爱去那里。

参考问题和答案：

1 Do you like to go to the park? What do you do there? (Ye
I like to take my dog to the park and play with her there.

2 Do you like to go to the cinema? (Yes, I love watching film
No, I am not too interested in films.)

yín háng

银行

你的城市有银行吗？你知道它在哪里吗？

参考问题和答案：

1 Have you ever been to a bank? Where is it? (Yes. It is on Garden Road./No, because I am too young to go.)

2 Are there many banks in your city? (Yes, because it is a big city./No, there are only two banks.)

Let's think

提醒学生对照第4至9页的内容完成题目。故事中没有提及消防局和教堂。

1 Which buildings are mentioned in the story? Put a tick or a cross.

2 Discuss other important public facilities with your friend. Paste your photos below and explain why they are important.

公共设施是由政府提供的、属于社会的、给公众享用或使用的公共建筑或设备。

城市里还要有……

Paste your photo here.

Paste your photo here.

城市里还要有游泳池，因为我们要多运动。

参考答案：
城市里还要有广场，因为人们可以在那里见朋友、听音乐。
城市里还要有美术馆，因为人们喜欢美术。

New words

 **1** Learn the new words.

延伸活动：
学生根据本页设计图简单描述这个社区。如：这个学校的东边
是公园，南边是火车站，西边是图书馆，北边是医院。

超市 SUPERMARKET

商店 SHOP

体育馆 GYMNASIUM

图书馆 LIBRARY

医院 HOSPITAL

邮局 POST OFFICE

公园 PARK

银行 BANK

学校 SCHOOL

设计

火车站 TRAIN STATION

电影院 CINEMA

或者

2 Listen to your teacher and point to the correct words above.

听听说说 Listen and say

🎧 03 **1** Listen carefully. Number the pictures.

🎧 04 **2** Look at the pictures. Listen to the story

我们一起去公园跑步。 2

我和弟弟在图书馆看书。 1

我们在电影院看电影。 3

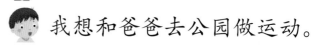

星期六，你们想去哪里？

我想和爸爸去公园做运动。

③

星期日呢？我们一起去体育馆看篮球比赛，好吗？

好！星期日见。

第一题录音稿：
上午，我和弟弟想去公园。但是因为外面下雨了，所以我们去图书馆看书了。下午，天气很好，我们一起去公园跑步。晚上，妈妈带我们去电影院看电影。我们今天很开心。

J.

星期六上午，我要和爱莎去图书馆看书。下午，我要和妈妈去超市买东西。

浩浩，别忘了，星期日我们要去医院看阿姨。

我怎么忘了呢？

第二题参考问题和答案：

Which places are mentioned in the story? (The park, the library, the supermarket, the gymnasium and the hospital.)

3 Look at the picture and complete the sentences. Write the letters.

a 医院　b 或者　c 超市　d 学校

提醒学生仔细看图，观察人物所在的建筑物是哪一种。

1　浩浩坐校车去 __d__ 。

2　因为伊森不舒服，所以他去 __a__ 了。

3　爱莎在 __c__ 门口，她想买巧克力 __b__ 饼干。

Task

延伸活动：

学生分三个小组，每个小组向全班介绍两种公共设施，内容尽量详细为佳。如：我们的城市有两家医院和三个公园。医院在城市的东边，我们可以坐汽车或者地铁去那里，很方便。三个公园在城市里不同的地方，公园里有很多树和很多花，很多人喜欢去那里休息和做运动。

How many public facilities are there in your neighbourhood? Research and discuss with your friend.

Public facility	学校	超市	医院	公园	邮局	体育馆
Number						

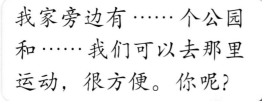

我家旁边有……个公园和……我们可以去那里运动，很方便。你呢？

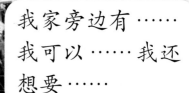

我家旁边有……我可以……我还想要……

Game

If you were a city designer, where would you build a bank in the city? Draw it on the map and discuss with your friend.

想一想，银行设计在哪里好呢？

我觉得银行可以在……旁边。因为那里有很多……从……到银行很方便。

Chant

延伸活动：
老师先准备歌词中提到的公共设施图片并分发给不同学生，
说唱时，拿照片的学生配合歌词逐一将它们高举起来。

🎧 **Listen and say.**

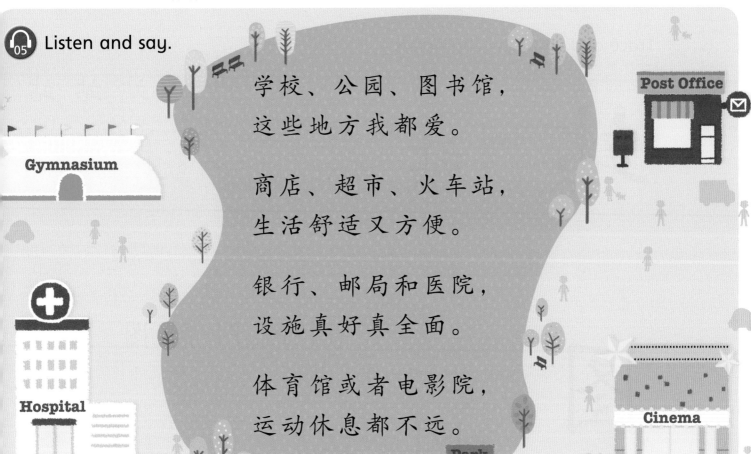

学校、公园、图书馆，
这些地方我都爱。

商店、超市、火车站，
生活舒适又方便。

银行、邮局和医院，
设施真好真全面。

体育馆或者电影院，
运动休息都不远。

生活用语 Daily expressions

我想去……或者……
I want to go to ... or ...

参考表述：
我想去超市买东西或者
去公园休息。

15

写一写 Write

1 Trace and write the characters.

` 丶 亠 六 立 立 立 站 站 站

站 站 站 站

丨 冂 冂 冈 冈 图 图 图
乛 乛 书 书

图 书 图 书

提醒学生不要忘记写"书"
字最后右上角的一点。

2 Write and say.

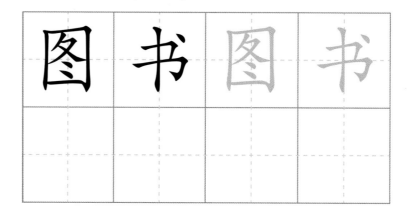
我想去 图书 馆看
书，你在哪里？

我在火车 站 。

3 Fill in the blanks with the correct words. Colour the books using the same colours.

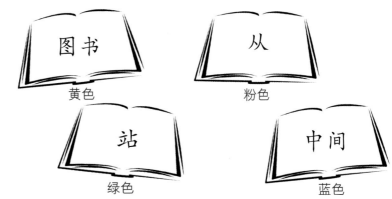

图书
黄色

从
粉色

站
绿色

中间
蓝色

"请问， 图书 馆在哪里？"女孩问。

"在火车 站 旁边，你可以 从 公共汽车 站 坐车去。"我说。

"是公园和邮局 中间 的车 站 吗？"女孩问。

"不是，是医院前面的车 站 。"我说。

拼音输入法 Pinyin input

Write the correct letters to complete the paragraph. Compete with your friends and see who can finish typing the paragraph first.

a 很漂亮

b 火车站旁边

c 这是北京火车站

你知道这是哪儿吗？ c 。
火车站的楼很高，从很远的地方
也可以看见它。 b 有一个公
园，里面有很多树和花， a ！
我们可以从北京火车站坐火车去
很多城市，非常方便。

延伸活动：
打完段落后，学生两人一组，互相检查对方是否有打错的字词，然后再大声朗读段落一次。

多元学习 Connections

Cultures

1 Learn about some classical public buildings around the world. Match the pictures to the descriptions and write the letters.

这些楼真漂亮。它们是什么呢？

这是图书馆还是邮局？你知道吗？

a Al-Qarawiyyin Library is in Morocco. It was built in the ninth century. It is one of the oldest libraries in the world.

b Kuala Lumpur Railway Station is in Malaysia. It was completed in 1910. The station is famous for its architecture.

c Hospital of the Holy Spirit is in Germany. It was built in 1332. It is one of the oldest hospitals in Europe.

中间的图容易选出是 b；左图建筑为西式风格，故选德国 c，右图建筑为伊斯兰教风格，故选摩洛哥 a。

2 Look at the pictures and compare the buildings. Tell your friend about the ones you like and say why.

图书馆

学校

我更喜欢上面的图书馆。因为那儿有很多树和草。

我更喜欢下面的学校。因为它的设计很……我觉得……

让学生说说他们所在城市的一些环保措施，也可鼓励学生上网搜寻环保做得特别出众的城市并与全班同学分享有关信息。如：冰岛政府在其首都大力推行地热（岛上温泉的水蒸气）和水力作为取暖和电力能源的措施，此外，还推动"百公里耗油量低于 5 升环保型汽车可以在市区免费停车"等环保活动。

1 Learn about environmentally friendly green cities. Match the pictures to the descriptions.

Solar panels absorb the sun's rays as a source of energy to generate electricity.

Bicycles are a form of sustainable transport. It does not use natural resources, but is cheap and efficient.

Windmills or wind turbines convert the energy in wind to generate electricity.

2 Design a green city of the future. You may use the icons. Talk about it with your friend.

绿色城市

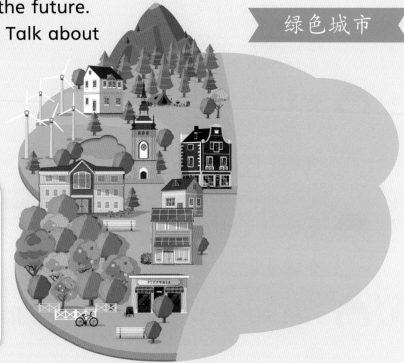

这是我设计的绿色城市。我们用风和太阳帮助城市发电。这里有很多树和公园。这里还有……

提醒学生先观察左边的设计，再在右边完成整个城市设计图。

19

1 Hao Hao and Ling Ling are going to visit a library. Read what they say and r

① 从学校到邮局，坐车要多长时间？

② 那很远。我想可能要三十分钟。

③ 你看，超市在路的左边，它真大。

④ 右边有医院，医院比超市远。

⑤ 我不喜欢去医院。我喜欢去公园或者体育馆，可以在那儿运动。

⑥ 那是火车 站 吗？我们快到 图书 馆了。

⑦ 是的。图书馆在前面，不远了。

⑧ 我们快到图书馆门口了。快去看看这个有趣的地方！

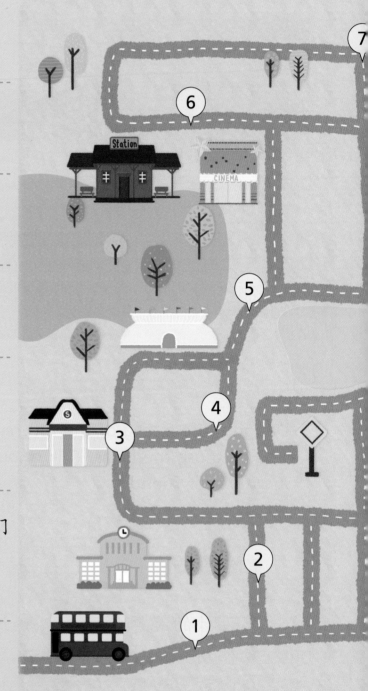

y with your friend.

2 Work with your friend. Colour the stars and the chillies.

Words and sentences	说	读	写
学校	☆	☆	🌶
图书馆	☆	☆	🌶
商店	☆	☆	🌶
超市	☆	☆	🌶
医院	☆	☆	🌶
火车站	☆	☆	☆
或者	☆	☆	🌶
公园	☆	☆	🌶
设计	☆	🌶	🌶
邮局	☆	🌶	🌶
体育馆	☆	🌶	🌶
电影院	☆	🌶	🌶
银行	☆	🌶	🌶
我们还可以设计体育馆、医院或者火车站。	☆	🌶	🌶
别忘了公园或者电影院。	☆	🌶	🌶

Talk about public buildings and facilities	☆

3 What does your teacher say?

 分享 Sharing

延伸活动：

1 学生用手遮盖英文，读中文单词，并思考单词意思；
2 学生用手遮盖中文单词，看着英文说出对应的中文单词；
3 学生两人一组，尽量运用中文单词复述第4至9页内容。

Words I remember

学校	xué xiào	school
图书馆	tú shū guǎn	library
商店	shāng diàn	shop
超市	chāo shì	supermarket
医院	yī yuàn	hospital
火车站	huǒ chē zhàn	train station
或者	huò zhě	either, or
公园	gōng yuán	park
设计	shè jì	to design
邮局	yóu jú	post office
体育馆	tǐ yù guǎn	gymnasium
电影院	diàn yǐng yuàn	cinema
银行	yín háng	bank

Other words

设计师	shè jì shī	designer
如果	rú guǒ	if
学习	xué xí	to learn
生活	shēng huó	life
让	ràng	to let
设施	shè shī	facility
全面	quán miàn	comprehensive
忘	wàng	to forget
大家	dà jiā	everybody
都	dōu	both, all
游泳池	yóu yǒng chí	swimming pool
舒适	shū shì	comfortable
发电	fā diàn	to generate electricity

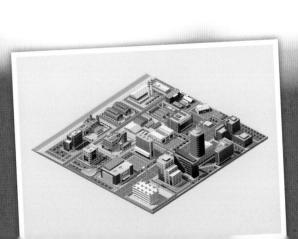

OXFORD
UNIVERSITY PRESS

Oxford University Press is a department of the University of Oxford.
It furthers the University's objective of excellence in research, scholarship,
and education by publishing worldwide. Oxford is a registered trade mark of
Oxford University Press in the UK and in certain other countries

Published in Hong Kong by
Oxford University Press (China) Limited
39th Floor, One Kowloon, 1 Wang Yuen Street, Kowloon Bay,
Hong Kong

© Oxford University Press (China) Limited 2017

The moral rights of the author have been asserted

First Edition published in 2017

Illustrated by Anne Lee, Emily Chan and Wildman

Photographs for reproduction permitted by Dreamstime.com

China National Publications Import & Export (Group) Corporation is an authorized distributor of
Oxford Elementary Chinese.

Please contact content@cnpiec.com.cn or 86-10-65856782

ISBN: 978-0-19-082308-5

10 9 8 7 6 5 4 3 2

Teacher's Edition
ISBN: 978-0-19-082320-7

10 9 8 7 6 5 4 3 2